THE GETAWAY

EXPERT ESCAPE & EVASION

by Jamie Pietras

with Tony and Jonna Mendez
Consultants

Scholastic Inc.
New York • Toronto • London • Auckland • Sydney
Mexico City • New Delhi • Hong Kong • Buenos Aires

ISBN 0-545-00080-7

Copyright © 2007 by Scholastic Inc.

Designer: Aruna Goldstein
Illustrations: James W. Elston
Comic Strip Illustrations: Yancey Labat

Photos: Page 17: Reuters/Corbis.

12 11 10 9 8 7 6 5 4 3 2 1

7 8 9 10 11/0

Printed in the U.S.A.

First printing, April 2007

The publisher has made every effort to ensure that the activities in this book are safe
when done as instructed. Children are encouraged to do their spy activities with willing
friends and family members and to respect others' right to privacy. Adults should
provide guidance and supervision whenever the activity requires.

Table of Contents

THE GREAT ESCAPE!

Picture this: You're on a secret mission and you've totally changed your name, your voice, and even the way you dress. You're deep in enemy territory when, *suddenly*—you've been figured out! Do you run? Do you hide? Never fear, secret agent. If you're like most good spies, you've already planned your getaway!

A good **escape and evasion plan** requires cutting-edge spy tools. More importantly, it requires secrecy and planning. After all, once a cover is blown, it's blown for good!

Think about the times you've needed to make a quick getaway. Maybe it was when you were playing hide-and-seek, or trying to avoid a school bully. You just never know when you need to disappear without a trace! Fortunately, with your latest **Ultimate Spy Club** handbook and spy kit, you'll learn about...

Emergency Escape Kits

You'll learn how to create your very own emergency escape kit using everyday items from around your house. You'll learn how to leave simple signals and how to build a compass from scratch!

Sneaking Around

You'll learn how to move without making a peep and sneak away without being noticed.

Getting Away!

You'll learn how to navigate unknown territory and come up with escape routes for any situation!

And more!

Be sure to visit the
Ultimate Spy Club online at:
www.scholastic.com/ultimatespy

This month's secret password is:
maketheescape

What's in Your *Spy Kit*?

Your spy kit contains two Ultimate Spy Club gadgets:

Spy Locator Keychain

This nifty gadget is built for secret agents like you. No matter where your adventures may lead, you'll never lose your sense of direction thanks to the tiny compass. Better yet, you can blow into it like a whistle to communicate with fellow spies. Then, press the button and you have a flashlight!

Signal Watch

This watch is tough enough to handle any spy situation. Press the button to project the Ultimate Spy Club signal to communicate with your co-spies. Take it with you wherever you go and you'll never be late for a secret rendezvous!

MISSION #1:
PLAN YOUR ESCAPE

If you've seen spies on TV, you know they're prepared for anything! When they're lost, they pull maps from out of the blue! When they need to switch disguises—presto! They're in a mustache and overcoat faster than you can blink an eye!

To react quickly to any situation, you have to plan ahead. Professional spies make emergency escape kits, so they're always ready if they need to make a quick getaway.

It's important to think of all the possible outcomes of a situation so you'll be ready no matter what happens. That's why you should always learn as much as you can. Then you'll always have a plan and a couple of backup plans!

Buggin' Out!

It's always important to plan ahead for whatever might happen. That's why professional spies keep all their escape equipment in something called an emergency escape kit or a **bug-out kit**. Don't squirm, though—most of the things you'll need for your kit are regular items from around your house. Here's a checklist of spy tools you'll need to get started.

⇨ **Tissues**. If you're ever taken prisoner, you can use tissues to write emergency messages! Practice at home. Just write a message in ink onto a tissue, roll it into a tiny ball, and pass it along to a friend!

⇨ **LED light**. These are the best kinds of lights to guide you through dark expeditions. Your Spy Locator Keychain has a small light. If you want even more power, you can pick up stronger **LED lights** at any camping store.

⇨ **Coins**. Coins can be used to make emergency phone calls. The edge of a dime or a penny can also be used like a little screwdriver.

⇨ **Local maps**. If you always keep a local map handy, you'll never be caught without an escape route!

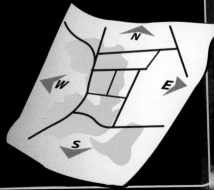

Small mirror. Mirrors reflect sunlight, so they're great for signaling other spies. Plus, you can always use a mirror to check what's around a corner.

Chalk. A pen won't get you very far if you need to write signals on streets or driveways. That's what chalk is for!

Whistle. What if your spy friends are in the next backyard and you need to tell them the coast is clear?

Try a whistle signal! You can use your Spy Locator Keychain to let your friends know that it's safe to come back to home base.

REAL SPY GADGETS

During World War II, U.S. spies developed a penny that contained a tiny blade. If they were ever caught and bound, they could use it to cut themselves free.

A Secret Stash

So, you've got your maps, coins, and other spy gear packed up in your bug-out kit. Mission accomplished, right? Wrong! Your job is far from over. You've got to keep your stash hidden! Pesky sisters and nosy neighbors are never far behind!

Spies call these hiding places **cache sites** (pronounced *cash*) or caches. If you've chosen your cache site wisely, you'll be the only one with access to your bug-out kit. Oh yeah... be sure to stash a granola bar or some chocolate, too. It's tough to make a getaway on an empty stomach!

When you hide your escape kit, pick a spot nobody would ever suspect—like the bushes in front of your home, or a cupboard nobody uses. Your cache site also needs to be somewhere you'll be able to access easily. If you can't get to your escape kit when you need it, it won't do you any good! If you hide your kit outside, make sure it's protected from rain and dirt by sealing it in a plastic bag.

SPY HISTORY uNcovEREd

During the Cold War, the KGB set up secret caches in cities all over the world. These caches held all sorts of things, like money, radios, and even weapons. That way their agents would have what they needed no matter what happened. Even though they were set up a long time ago, a lot of people think these abandoned caches are still hidden around the world!

Camo Cover

What's a good way to make sure you get away? Make sure no one sees you! Want to learn how to really blend in? Then it's time to invest in some **camouflage**!

Color Me Hidden!

Camouflage comes in different colors: brown, beige, and tan for the desert, and green and black for the jungle. If you're just gearing up for a game of hide-and-seek, pick colors that match the bushes and trees in your neighborhood.

Once you're suited up, smear a little bit of dark makeup or mud on your face and hands. If that's too messy, just put on a dark hat and gloves. A bunch of leaves added to your clothes will make you even harder to spot!

You should always try to conceal yourself as well as possible. If you need to hide out in the open, try to lie in the shadow of a tree or a garage. More importantly, keep still. Remember, never hide anywhere you don't have permission to be. And always use the buddy system to tell a friend where you're hiding.

SPY HISTORY uNcovEREd

When the United States Navy Seals train for hiding, they'll spend hours or even days without moving an inch!

Walk Stealthily

The best getaway artists are like ninjas—they walk without making a peep! But you don't have to be a black belt to learn how to tiptoe like a professional.

Whether you want to sneak away from a bossy brother or become the best hide-and-seek player on your block, check out these tips from the masters.

⇨ **Tip #1: Scope out the scene!**
If you know where you're going, you'll know what to avoid!

⇨ **Tip #2: Dress for the occasion!**
Wear dark clothes and pick shoes that don't have loud, clunky bottoms. Sneakers usually do the trick—the darker the better.

⇨ **Tip #3: Wait for a distraction!**
Plan your movements around breezes, traffic, or other kinds of noisy distractions. Someone started vacuuming in the other room? Perfect! Make your escape.

⇨ **Tip #4: Breathe easy!**
Easy does it—try to relax so that your breaths are slow and soft.

Tip #5: Soften your steps!

Walk slowly and be extra careful not to step on anything that might make noise, like a twig or dry, crunchy leaves. It's a good idea to feel a spot with your toes before you take a step.

Tip #6: Freeze!

If you hear somebody coming, stand still! Even the slightest movement can mean the difference between "mission accomplished" and "mission failed!"

Tip #7: Be Patient!

Patience separates real spies from amateurs. Spy survival is not about getting to your destination the fastest, it's about getting there *without getting caught.*

More Than Meets the Eye

Trying to steer clear of an older brother? Caught up in a serious game of chase? Sometimes, the best way to get somebody off your trail is to send your pursuer down another path entirely. You can do this by using a **decoy**. A decoy is any person, object, or situation used to be mistaken for something else. Here are a couple of secret tricks if you ever want to use decoys for your own getaways.

The Dummy

It's amazing what you can pull off with some clothes and a few newspapers for stuffing. That's right, smarty—it's dummy time! You can build your own dummy the same way you'd make a scarecrow. Just stuff some crumpled-up newspaper into one of your shirts and a pair of pants. You can even throw on your favorite hat. Prop it up on a chair and it will look like you never left the room!

The False Trail

Footprints are one of the worst things a spy can leave behind—that is, unless the footprints are really a decoy! If you're ever walking through mud, snow, or sand, you can leave fake footprints

by walking in one direction, and then retracing your steps backwards. Fake trails work really well if you can build them next to a grassy area or some other place where you can get away without leaving footprints.

The Nose Knows

Sometimes counterspies will try to catch real-life secret agents by sending dogs to follow their scent. If you make a fake trail and cross it, the dog will become confused about which way you went, because your scent will go in four different directions. Cross your trail several times to add to the confusion!

The Accomplice

If your enemy knows you're wearing blue jeans, a red coat, and a green cap, he has a pretty good idea of what to watch out for. But that doesn't mean you need to get caught. You can actually use this to your advantage if you've got a

Group Getaway

If you're with your group of fellow spies and you're being followed, try a **starburst** to confuse your enemy. A starburst is when you and two or more co-spies quickly split up and head in different directions. Whoever's after you will have to decide who to follow.

REAL SPY GADGETS

When the CIA wanted to fool Russian spies during the 1950s, they created a pop-up dummy called a JIB, short for Jack-in-the-Box. They would seat the JIB in the front seat of a car where a real CIA agent was supposed to be sitting. Counterspies who were following behind wouldn't be able to tell the difference between the JIB and the real person they were looking for!

co-spy working with you. All you need to do is have your co-spy meet you in a prearranged place like a park or a schoolyard and swap coats and hats. When the enemy thinks he's found you, he'll actually find your friend instead.

THE COLDITZ ESCAPE ACADEMY

Colditz Castle was a German high-security prison during World War II, full of soldiers who had escaped from regular prisons. Putting together so many clever, crafty minds created a group of escape experts who were later called The Colditz Escape Academy. They made 300 escape attempts, 130 of which were successful!

In one of the successful escape attempts, decoys were key! A group of Dutch prisoners noticed a manhole cover they were able to open. Prisoners would climb into the underground sewer and wait. When the coast was clear, they'd climb out and slip over the wall. But the prison guards counted the prisoners four times a day. How did the Dutch keep the Germans from noticing the missing prisoners? They made dummies! One of the prisoners was a sculptor. He made realistic heads that were then placed on top of prison uniforms. The prisoners would hold the dummies up between them so the prisoner count wouldn't change.

Backup!

ROAD CLOSED

Most spies live by a rule known as Murphy's Law: What can go wrong, will go wrong! Since no escape strategy is foolproof, it always pays to have a backup plan.

If the escape route you've mapped out leads you to a locked gate, there's no need to panic—*if* you've got an alternate route. If you've agreed to discuss your secret plans on somebody's porch but find it swarming with adults, you can meet at your backup spot instead.

Mission Aborted!

In the spy game, there are three golden rules: First, there is no operation that can't be cancelled. Second, there is nothing you can do wrong that can't be fixed. The third and most important rule is to always go with your gut! Even the best spies have to cut their losses sometimes, so if something feels wrong, it probably is.

POP Culture

When your plans really fall through, it doesn't hurt to have a grappling gun! In the movie *Alex Rider: Operation Stormbreaker*, the 14-year-old British spy Alex Rider finds himself being chased. He escapes by using a grappling hook to snag a helicopter for a ride!

Danger Zone

Since plans can fall through, it's important that spies have a way to let their co-spies know that their plans have changed, or that they're in danger. That's when danger signals come into play.

Special Signals

There are a lot of different ways to say "Danger!" without actually saying a word. Did you know that...

➡ In Europe, straw is a universal sign of danger. Many Europeans hang straw from icy bridges as a warning not to cross, or on fences that house dangerous animals like dogs or bulls.

➡ When the United States Army and Navy want to say, "trouble ahead," they fly an American flag upside down.

19

Boy Scouts and Girl Scouts have their own special danger signals. They simply arrange things in threes. Three stacked coins or three flashes of a mirror could mean "watch out!"

REAL SPY GADGETS

Search-and-rescue teams still consider signal mirrors one of the best ways of communicating. People use signal mirrors to send out a series of flashes of light. These flashes can be detected from miles away!

Your Own Secret Signal!

Think about the ways you might signal danger in your neighborhood. You could draw a secret symbol in chalk that only you and your friends understand. You could use your Spy Locator Keychain to send out three flashes of light or whistle blasts, or project the Ultimate Spy Club signal from your Signal Watch. Or you could pick some other object, like grass, that only your spy team would recognize as a sign of trouble ahead! The more creative you get, the better your signal will be!

SPY HISTORY uNcovEREd

Oleg Gordievsky was a KGB officer, secretly working for British intelligence. He passed along important Soviet secrets for eleven years. Eventually he was exposed, and Gordievsky knew the KGB was watching him closely. In 1985, Gordievsky decided that he needed to escape to England before he was arrested.

Gordievsky had already arranged a danger signal with British intelligence. All he had to do was stand on a certain street corner holding a shopping bag from a famous British store at a certain time. A British intelligence officer drove by, spotted him, and knew that their escape plan was going into effect.

Tap Code

Tap code is a special code that can be used by two captured spies to communicate with each other. It uses a series of taps, and prisoners often used it to communicate by tapping on the wall that separated them from their co-spies.

	1	2	3	4	5
1	A	B	C	D	E
2	F	G	H	I	J
3	L	M	N	O	P
4	Q	R	S	T	U
5	V	W	X	Y	Z

Take a look at the grid. The numbers stand for the number of taps you make, and the letters are the letters of the message you're sending. There are 26 letters in the alphabet, but only 25 spaces in the grid, so if you need to use the letter *K*, just use *C* instead.

To use the code, find the letter you need on the chart. If your first letter was *P*, you'd see that *P* is in the 5th column (columns go down) and the 3rd row (rows go across). So, to tap the letter *P*, you'd tap 5 times, wait a second, then tap 3 times.

When listening to tap code, it's best to write down the number of taps you hear first. Then you can use your notes and the grid to figure out the secret message.

SPY HISTORY uNCovEREd

The tap code was invented during World War II. It was used again by American prisoners during the Vietnam War. One special message they would sometimes tap to one another was "GNST," which stood for, "Good night, sleep tight."

MISSION #2: GETTING AROUND

So, you're a master of your neighborhood and you know every single nook and cranny. That doesn't mean squat if you're sent to a new location—like your cousin's neighborhood!

What happens if you need to find a hiding place in a park you've never been to? What happens if you have to fend for yourself in a strange store, library, or playground? A map and a compass are great to have, but you need to know what to do when you don't have these key things with you.

There are ways to make your own compass, tell direction from the world around you, and make sure you're always noticing key landmarks. Better grab a flashlight and a notepad—it's time to do some exploring!

X Marks the Spot

Maps and locals are very helpful when it comes to learning about new places. Fortunately, they're pretty easy to find. Still, the maps and people you find won't tell you everything. That's why you need to do some mapping of your own. Take notes about the different buildings, bus or subway stops, and busy streets you want to stay away from. Never be afraid to ask for directions, and pay attention to the locals when you do. How do they speak? How do they dress? The more you know about them, the more you can fit in!

Mysterious Mapping

Sometimes, a map can give you away. After all, locals don't need maps! If you have the kind of tissue paper that's used to wrap gifts, you can make your own secret spy map.

REAL SPY GADGETS

During World War II, spies developed a special set of playing cards. Each card peeled back to reveal part of a map. When all of the cards were put together, a getaway map was formed!

SPY HISTORY UNCOVERED

During World War II, U.S. spies drew maps on small pieces of silk and stitched them right into their clothes! The silk was so thin, the enemy never noticed!

Finding North

If you keep your Spy Locator Keychain with you at all times, you'll always be able to figure out which way is north. But what happens if you don't have your **compass** with you? Should you just follow your nose? Not quite—but your nose will help. First, you need a simple sewing needle, and then a little "nose oil." Confused? Grossed out? Read on…

Have an adult help you take an ordinary sewing needle and rub one side of it against a magnet in one direction a few dozen times. This will make the needle become magnetized, just like the needle in your compass. This means that it will always point to the north.

A compass is nothing more than a **magnetized needle** that floats on a small amount of water. To get your needle to float, rub your finger against the side

of your nose a few times and then rub your finger on the unmagnetized end of the needle. That way, it will pick up the natural oils it needs to stay on top of the water's surface. Or, you can stick the needle into a small piece of cork, and place the cork in the water.

If you have a cup of water or find a small puddle, all you have to do is place the needle on top, and you have a compass that points north!

REAL SPY GADGETS

Spies have all kinds of clever compasses. Famous spy gadget designer Clayton Hutton designed tiny compasses that could be hidden inside buttons, pens, cuff links, and more!

Into the Wilderness

There are other ways of figuring out directions without using a compass. The world around you has a ton of clues, if you know where to look.

When you're surrounded by nothing but trees, everything can start to look the same. Always bring your Spy Locator Keychain along and be extra careful to take notes about the landmarks around you. Pay special attention to the big hills, streams, and any trees or plants that are unique or weird. Remember where you found them, and leave bright markers either in the ground or on trees to indicate where you've already been.

No Compass? No Problem!

If you don't have your compass, here are a few quick tricks to help you figure out which way is north.

➡ Try to find a tree with moss growing on it. Why? Moss always grows on the north side of trees. Once you know which way is north, you can determine the other **cardinal directions**—south (the opposite direction), east (to the right), and west (to the left).

If there are no trees in sight, pay close attention to the time and your shadow. If you're on a lunchtime mission (around noon), look for the direction in which shadows are cast. That's north! If it's later in the day and the sun is setting, shadows point to the east. During a rising sun early in the morning, shadows point to the west.

POP Culture

In the movie *Finding Nemo*, Marlin and Dory have to navigate their way to Sydney in order to get to Nemo. All the while, Nemo is plotting his own escape plan!

SPY TIP:

When you're exploring out in the woods, you have to be extra careful. First, you should never go without an adult. Second, you should always tell someone back at home base when you're leaving and when you'll be back.

Star Light, Star Bright

Some of the most important spy missions take place after dark. If you don't have your compass, it's pretty tough to find trees, and you're definitely not going to see any shadows. Fortunately, one of the most reliable maps appears when the sun goes down. That's right—when all else fails, you can always turn to the sky!

The North Star

Just look for the **Big Dipper** and the **Little Dipper**! Both of these constellations (pronounced kon-stuh-LAY-shuhns) can help you determine directions no matter where you are in the world!

Start with the Little Dipper. Can you find the star at the end of the "handle?" That's the North Star! Since this star always appears in the north part of the sky, you can determine which way is south, east, and west!

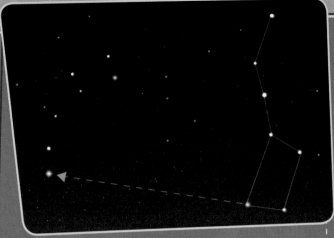

Now, find the Big Dipper. Do you see the two stars at the front of the "scoop" or "ladle" part of the constellation? They line up directly with the North Star! Finding the Big Dipper is an easy way to find the North Star.

The North Star is also called Polaris. People have been using the North Star to navigate for hundreds of years. Once you've found the North Star, you should keep your eye on it to make sure you're always going in the right direction. Imagine how much you'll impress your family and friends when you can figure out directions without a compass!

Watch the Rotation

Just like the moon and the sun, stars rise in the east and set in the west. If you watch the sky for about an hour, you'll be able to see where stars rise and fall. Once you've figured it out, simply stretch your right arm to where they are rising and your left arm to where they are falling. Now, you're looking toward the north!

SPY HISTORY UNCOVERED

Slaves in the American South called the Big Dipper the Drinking Gourd. They'd use the constellation to help them find the North Star, then follow it north, where they could escape to freedom.

Southern Spies

Spies living in the Southern Hemisphere can't use the North Star to guide them, because it's only visible in the Northern Hemisphere. In the Southern Hemisphere, people use another constellation—the Southern Cross—to help them navigate. The constellation is formed by four bright stars. The long line of the cross is formed by the two guiding stars. If you imagine that line continues five times its length toward the earth, you'll end up at a spot in the direction of south.

Nobody was better at navigating the outdoors than Native Americans. That's because they read their environment for clues about where they were. When they were in the desert, they knew they were west of the Rockies. If they saw high rugged mountains, they knew they were in the northwest. Green rolling mountains meant they were in the east or south.

You can use these same kinds of tricks in your own neighborhood. If you see "School Crossing" signs, you know you're coming up on a school. If you see ducks, you might be near a pond.

Mission ACCOMPLISHED!

Congratulations! You've learned how to figure out directions without a compass, lots of different danger signals, and even created your own personal escape kit! Be sure to put your Signal Watch and your Spy Locator Keychain someplace safe. And remember, always cover your tracks! The more you practice your spy techniques, the better you'll get—so grab some friends and teach them what you've learned. Good luck!

JAMIE PIETRAS
Writer

Jamie lives in New York City, where he works as a writer. When he wants to put on a spy disguise, he grows a mustache.

TONY AND JONNA MENDEZ
Consultants

Tony and Jonna spent their careers at the CIA. They worked overseas protecting American spies and the foreign assets working for the U.S. government. They were specialists in disguise and documents. Tony Mendez was named as one of the CIA's top spies in the last 50 years.

Glossary

These are the spy terms you need to know if you want to be a successful escape artist!

Big Dipper – A constellation that can be used to determine which way is north

Bug-Out Kit – A container that includes all of the tools and gadgets spies need to make successful escapes

Cache Site – A long-term hiding place

Camouflage – Clothing that is designed to blend in with an environment

Cardinal Directions – North, south, east, and west are the cardinal directions that can be determined by using a compass

Compass – A device that contains a magnet that always points north

Decoy – Any prop or situation that is used to distract or trick a person

Escape and Evasion Plan – A plan that spies design and rely upon to get out of dangerous situations

Jack-in-the-Box – A type of decoy in which a pop-up dummy is used to represent a spy

LED Light – A type of light that is useful for outdoor exploration

Little Dipper – A constellation that can be used to determine which way is north

Magnetized Needle – A special type of needle used in a compass

Starburst – When three or more spies split up and take off in different directions